SUCCESSORIES®

WHAT IS HAPPINESS?

397 of the best answers from the young, the old, and the wise.

Compiled by Sharon Post and Ollie Peacock

SUCCESSORIES LIBRARY

For information, write Successories® Publishing, 919 Springer Drive, Lombard, Illinois 60148-6416. Telephone (708) 953-8440.

Book Design: Eric Zeigler and Sandra Chlebek

ISBN: 1-880461-34-X

1 2 3 4 5 6 7 8 Printing/QPK/Year 99 98 97 96 95

10/31/95

TO JIM & CORL:

You've given me thousands of reasons to be happy.

Thank you.

Tanja

♡

INTRODUCTION

It all started in Sarasota, Florida last year when I asked a party of fourteen, while having dinner, to finish the sentence "Happiness is..."

After losing two close relatives, I was trying to work my way out of a very depressed feeling. Knowing I had to think positive to do this, I started thinking of all the happy times we had shared. The happiness these two loved ones had been responsible for, always giving, never taking.

As my mind wandered, I wondered what happiness meant to most people. Was it wealth, success, or just the simple love of family and friends?

I decided to ask the very young, the middle aged, and the very old. I visited preschools, high schools, nursing homes, even the "man on the street." Ages from 3 to 102 shared their reasons for happiness and, to my delight, all ages said, "Being with my family," "The love of God," and even "A little puppy."

After talking with several hundred folk, I realized that happiness is "Happy Memories." We can all build them.

ACKNOWLEDGEMENTS

Our heartfelt appreciation to our families who helped tremedously in gathering quotes for this book. Our grateful thanks to all who contributed to this collection. *Southland Nursing Home, McIntosh High, Sandy Creek High, Flat Rock High, Huddleston Elementary, Melody Bremer, Lynn Wallace, Barbara Serapion, Hank Rast, Cynde Snider, Amy Ernest, Lura Landis, Donna McDaniel, B.J. Hays, Lucia Beatenbough, JoAnn Blake, Mr. White, Ms. Sconyers, Tracy Mandel, Gladys Hallwood, Merkel Ludwig, Billy Jean Milsap, Roy Adams, Martha Wight, Frances Brim, Andrew Prince, Cindy Cooper, Charlie Coursey, Sammy Rowland, Debbie Rowland, Charles Mansour, Kevin Breen, Dorothy, Nit, Fred, Joan, Jamie, Jay McInvale, Scott Peacock, Robbie Peacock, Christopher Hurt, Carmen Moore, Carla Post, Dora, Connie Elaine, Alicia, Chezz McCain, Adam Macy, Mary Moore, Stuart Edward, Brittany, Jeffery, Cindy Bowers, Lori Franklin, Fran, Charlie Coursey, Rick Nelson, Rosa Neil, Rubie Post, Bill Peacock, Tracy Bell, Bob Peacock, Cynthia Wade, Doris Henley, Tom Weldon, Stephen Miller, Katie Thompson, Shawn Exum, Johnnie Wyler, Lottie Meadows, Andrea Laine Prince, Mike Merrick, Dawson Dees, Harold Mack, Lucile Powell, Ree Green, Joy Adams, Sheila Geist, Jennifer, Cheri, Charles McInvale, Bill Powell, Mrs. Tracy Baggs, Josh Stephens, Tiffany Steele, Joel, Troy Stone, Melanie, Carl Tyler Prince, Omie Gibson, Wendy Wilson, Matthew, Robyn, Jeff Powell, Mavis Peacock, Miranda, Joseph Hyde, Eric Sorenson, Greg Wilson, Dora, Roy Adams, Emitt Brown, Ruth Greenway, Mary Moore, Ann Oakey, Aaron, Brandon Bailey, Christy Mitchell, Josh Teal, Alicia, Bryan, Billy Hendrix, Carl Post, George Coursey, Dwight, Jean, Osamu, Russ Mann, Walter Mast, Lila, Sally Kirkland, Sopheia, Nancy Hall, Lisley, Laura, Marjorie, Howard Wall, Marsha, Glorie Meems, Heida Sims, Gurtha Coursey, Faye Dennis, Nina Smothers, Kevin, Tayler, Linda Merrieweather, Linda Croft,*

ACKNOWLEDGEMENTS

Mandy, Chrystal, Jody, Margaret Cross, James Adler, Charlene Brown, Audrey Henley, Elaine Ruskin, Linda O'Neal, Elaine Hare, Lyvone, Tanya, T. Ashlei Prez-ball, Patricia Wilson, Amy Palmer, Mark Delheart, Blake MacFarlan, Natalie, Dickey, Annalynn, Kimberly, Heather Carlisle, Meliss White, Kate Joiner, Bill Kidwell, John Herber, Shirly Hardcastle, Annette Pike, Reba Thopson, Johnnie Gentry, J.W. Harrison, Rubin Knowles, Don Potratz, Ken Leonard, Dave Cantrell, Jared Cantrell, Karen Woodley, Christy Chauncey, Jennifer Mengel, Dana Rick, Justin Bishop, Leslie Thomas, Scott Maloney, Russell Long, Jessica Knight, Charlott Lewis, Tim Peacock, Debra Kerri, Cynthia Houser, Bev Patty, Theresa Young, Raymond Patty, Kandva LaShore, Mr. Brown, Cosandra, Kara Pajewski, Paulette Gates, Lisa Thomas, Patricia Reese, Betty Smith, Shon Willis, Elouise Garner, Floyd Baldree, Eunice Douglas, Marcile Griffen, Joyce Jones, Dee Foster, Florence Burk, Chris Hunt, Donna Putman, Michele Putman, Bill Candy, Jim Brown, Charles Woods, Cheryl N. Whatley, Barbara Sall, Sheila Price, Ron Clover, Justin Clover, Becca Ross, Brent Smart, Janine Horsley, Chris Dolce, Sharon Mays, Christal, Stochura, Courtney Bryant, Reiko, Nicole Hester, Jason Miller, Stephanie Egeland, Pete Kelley, Tammitha Prince, Kelley Powell, Billy Powell, Sara Freeman, Jennifer Hill, Brenda Maddox, Brandi Bryson, Billy Merrit, Bill Phipps, Jeff Callahan, Michael Gilbert, Ashley Exum, Stephanie Boone, Casey Allen, Ryan Mitchell, Robert Hegginbotham.

A very special thanks to Curtis Edwards for his contribution in getting this book compiled.

In Memory of Pete and Kitty Kelley.

Happiness is…

singing, laughter, joy and friends.

— Age 87 —

friends, family and being with someone you love.

— Age 10 —

to someday go on a date with Cindy Crawford.

— Age 9 —

forty-five years with my husband.

— Age 77 —

Happiness is...

reading a good book and playing pikino.

— Age 95 —

someone surprising me with something.

— Age 86 —

seeing a rainbow in the sky.

— Age 28 —

being able to swim without arm floaties anymore.

— Age 9 —

Happiness is...

a bowl of popcorn, a cozy fire,
an old movie with someone you care
about on a stormy night.

— Age 26 —

to be able to pay all my bills.

— Age 36 —

working with my daughter.

— Age 67 —

Happiness is...

a little puppy.

— Age 4 —

a grandchild at play.

— Age 90 —

well, toys make me happy.

— Age 4 —

my sister, my dog, and my cat,
maybe not in that order.

— Age 9 —

Happiness is...

all things running smoothly.

— Age 19 —

health – love of my children.

— Age 32 —

getting a big cinnamon-roll at school.

— Age 10 —

leaving your purse in a grocery cart
and going back and finding it still there.

— Age 52 —

Happiness is…

serving as mayor for ten years.

— Age 68 —

never having to change a diaper again.

— Age 35 —

going to the circus on a rainy day.

— Age 13 —

most of all having God
as my personal savior.

— Age 51 —

Happiness is...

getting engaged.

— Age 19 —

never having to say I'm sorry.

— Age 18 —

seeing a baby take their first steps.

— Age 24 —

passing my driver's test with flying colors on the very first try.

— Age 17 —

Happiness is...

my daughter's love.

— Age 67 —

having my parents like my boyfriend.

— Age 17 —

knowing how to forgive.

— Age 48 —

getting the prom dress
that I have dreamed about.

— Age 18 —

Happiness is...

running and chasing boys.

— Age 5 —

seeing a rainbow in the sky.

— Age 19 —

never having to diet again.

— Age 4 —

a big fish in the lake
spitting golf balls back to me.

— Age 29 —

Happiness is…

spending a lifetime with the one I love.

— Age 89 —

playing war with my brother.

— Age 5 —

to get well.

— Age 87 —

always having someone to talk things over with.

— Age 76 —

Happiness is...

when my sisters aren't around.

— Age 9 —

vacationing with my wife.

— Age 50 —

finding out that you are
about to have your very first baby.

— Age 22 —

eating corn on the cobb.

— Age 5 —

Happiness is...

soccer, baseball, Nintendo,
and getting my brother in trouble.

— Age 10 —

having a cricket land in your hand
just as you run out of fish bait.

— Age 50 —

having my house clean by
Friday afternoon.

— Age 35 —

Happiness is...

awakening to a new day and
feeling good about it.

— Age 77 —

having my whole family pull together
and never holding a grudge.

— Age 65 —

where you are at the present.

— Age 82 —

never having to go to school again.

— Age 15 —

Happiness is...

having someone to love and share love with.

— Age 48 —

the 1996 Olympics.

— Age 12 —

being asked to the prom by the one boy whom I really wanted to ask me.

— Age 17 —

sliding down a slide.

— Age 3 —

Happiness is...

when I see my mom and dad
showing that they really
love me and each other.

— Age 14 —

catching a fish so big that it pulls
me in the lake.

— Age 14 —

fishing all day and telling the biggest
fish story later.

— Age 50 —

Happiness is...

playing putt-putt with Am Maw.

— Age 5 —

the joy of the first time my grandchild called me Am Maw.

— Age 45 —

learning to ride a bicycle.

— Age 12 —

looking through the eyes of my children – health and contentment with life.

— Age 38 —

Happiness is...

peace among people.

— Age 24 —

seeing your children with a happy life.

— Age 60 —

looking for the good, rather than
the bad, in people.

— Age 26 —

a rainy day in the desert.

— Age 16 —

Happiness is...

a child's first steps.

— Age 28 —

taking a sick child's temperature and finding it normal.

— Age 33 —

having a perfect newborn baby placed in your arms.

— Age 26 —

having a wife as pretty as she is sweet.

— Age 32 —

Happiness is...

finishing college and Alabama football.

— Age 24 —

a shiny yesterday, a sunny today,
and a bright tomorrow.

— Age 17 —

a vacation in Panama City, Florida.

— Age 15 —

helping others.

— Age 22 —

Happiness is...

teaching students who want to learn.

— Age 30 —

knowing where you stand with people and feeling secure in your relationship.

— Age 16 —

no pollution.

— Age 11 —

the true objective of life.

— Age 16 —

Happiness is…

knowing my family is well and that they trust in the Lord.

— Age 66 —

a peaceful day when there are no worries, no stress, and nothing to care about but being happy.

— Age 17 —

what you make it.

— Age 16 —

Happiness is...

being content to stare at the clouds for hours, making shapes out of the contrasting blue and white sky.

— Age 18 —

having fun, relaxing, and enjoying yourself.

— Age 25 —

going to the mall with my mom and having her surprise me by letting me pick out the outfit I want, instead of the one she wants me to have.

— Age 15 —

Happiness is…

finding your six pound, seventeen year-old puppy unharmed after he has fallen from a two story deck.

— Age 59 —

winning student council president.

— Age 10 —

a feeling you have when someone or something touches your heart with warmth– it makes you relax.

— Age 32 —

Happiness is...

having fun in all that you do.

— Age 40 —

getting circus tickets and watching the clowns fall down.

— Age 9 —

the ability to make someone laugh.

— Age 14 —

helping others achieve their goals for the future.

— Age 16 —

Happiness is...

the feeling you get when you do something nice and considerate for someone less fortunate.

— Age 19 —

not having lunchroom duty.

— Age 12 —

a place we spend our lives trying to find, when we realize we took it with us on the way.

— Age 19 —

Happiness is...

my girlfriend saying that she really cares about me.

— Age 16 —

chocolate chip cookies.

— Age 5 —

communication with God.

— Age 59 —

the essence of being in love, to cry and ponder over every little thing we cherish.

— Age 17 —

Happiness is...

spending the night with my grandmother and eating cereal in the middle of the night.

— Age 8 —

being proud of who you are and being able to speak your mind.

— Age 16 —

sleeping peacefully at night.

— Age 15 —

the love of my grandchildren.

— Age 45 —

Happiness is…

just like love – I need it, you need it, and we all need it to make our life complete.

— Age 29 —

your childhood friend calling just to say "Hi" after an absence of 20 years.

— Age 59 —

finding your pet that has been lost all night.

— Age 8 —

my daughter saying, "You're my friend."

— Age 67 —

Happiness is...

the joy for all the people who are smiling and running around outside.

— Age 55 —

eating tacos.

— Age 5 —

being alive – the love for each other.

— Age 74 —

being loved by somebody who loves you just the way you are.

— Age 24 —

Happiness is...

when you have a good life.

— Age 16 —

a sunny day in the desert.

— Age 25 —

when a boy gets his first puppy.

— Age 8 —

front row tickets to your favorite musical group.

— Age 16 —

Happiness is…

having no trouble finding
a date for the weekend.

— Age 22 —

life filled with lots of good times.

— Age 29 —

self ambition and having a heart
full of goodness.

— Age 31 —

living life to its fullest.

— Age 54 —

Happiness is…

eating an Arby's roast beef sandwich and knowing you have two more in the bag.

— Age 17 —

peace on earth.

— Age 62 —

*having three wishes, money,
a sports car, and three more wishes.*

— Age 17 —

running through a field of poppy plants.

— Age 19 —

Happiness is...

walking up a glistening waterfall in the mountains.

— Age 22 —

setting a table with a full candlelight dinner with someone you love.

— Age 28 —

being able to do what you want, when you want, and without a higher being telling you what to do.

— Age 15 —

Happiness is...

having people care about you and then showing it towards you.

— Age 47 —

the ocean on a beautiful day.

— Age 36 —

having fun, not having any worries on your mind, being free, and when it feels like you're floating around on a cloud.

— Age 14 —

Happy

Happiness is...

meeting someone with a genuine smile.

— Age 17 —

when it is my birthday and holidays.

— Age 9 —

knowing you have friends
to turn to whenever you need help.

— Age 34 —

making a birthday cake that turns out perfect.

— Age 51 —

Happiness is...

working with my mother.

— Age 44 —

the absence of sadness, having lots of friends and family that love you.

— Age 20 —

finding God's will for your life and realizing the love and forgiveness he showers upon you.

— Age 41 —

Happiness is...

feeling like you can do anything without having anyone judging you.

— Age 14 —

knowing that nothing could be better than knowing your true self and loving others more than yourself.

— Age 25 —

to see your daughter completely well after a terrible accident.

— Age 67 —

Happiness is…

sharing an ice cream cone with my six pound, seventeen year-old Pekingese.

— Age 37 —

the Braves winning the World Series.

— Age 26 —

talking and laughing.

— Age 13 —

when you have a lot of friends and are happy with your life.

— Age 9 —

Happiness is...

having an ample supply of food on hand when an unexpected snow storm hits the south.

— Age 46 —

writing a column for fifteen years, and when newcomers move into town saying your column made them feel right at home.

— Age 66 —

when you have nice parents.

— Age 5 —

Happiness is…

the knowledge that I can talk
with the Lord.

— Age 80 —

hearing the birds sing, seeing the sunshine
after a rain storm, smelling the honeysuckle,
making a child smile, a hug, a kiss.

— Age 33 —

when you can wake up in a free country.

— Age 29 —

Happiness is…

when people are nice to me, going to parties, and when Christmas comes.

— Age 9 —

playing, being with your family,
being loved by your family,
especially at holidays.

— Age 42 —

when my children are doing really well and are happy with their lives.

— Age 53 —

Happiness is...

when I score the winning goal in the finals of the soccer state championship with about thirty seconds to go.

— Age 15 —

the feeling you get when you touch out your opponent and win an Olympic gold medal.

— Age 18 —

something that can only be found within.

— Age 33 —

Happiness is...

treasure that can make the poorest man rich beyond imagination.

— Age 17 —

sleeping in a really cold bed with loads of goose feathers and talking on the phone on a really stormy night.

— Age 16 —

the first lick of an ice cream cone on a hot summer day.

— Age 16 —

Happiness is…

achieving a life-long goal that leaves you at a successful point, but knowing that you accomplished it by yourself.

— Age 66 —

walking in the summer rain, feeling it splash on your face and feeling the mud at your feet.

— Age 17 —

playing the piano, music of all kinds.

— Age 77 —

Happiness is...

not having to search for it.

— Age 50 —

having confidence in your publisher.

— Age 48 —

peace, quiet and unity of the world.

— Age 25 —

the birds, the bees, the flowers, the trees,
and a milk shake with fries.

— Age 13 —

Happiness is...

being able to give to someone in need.

— Age 71 —

not being afraid of the dark.

— Age 7 —

being loved for yourself.

— Age 45 —

going to Mt. McKinley and
actually seeing the top.

— Age 59 —

Happiness is...

throwing snowballs in July in Wyoming.

— Age 26 —

recovering your false teeth
after leaving them in a hotel room.

— Age 59 —

a spoon of peanut butter before going to bed.

— Age 7 —

looking on the bright side – taking your
troubles to the Lord and leaving them there.

— Age 82 —

Happiness is...

a satisfying burp after a good meal.

— Age 50 —

answering the phone to hear your child's voice a thousand miles away.

— Age 60 —

good friendship and good company.

— Age 28 —

looking at old home movies even if they are silent.

— Age 90 —

a husband who kisses me goodbye in the morning and hello in the evening, with love in his eyes.

— Age 41 —

hearing your husband tell someone you are a good cook.

— Age 67 —

salvation found in Jesus.

— Age 24 —

Happiness is...

when you look for the good in someone
or something and find it.

— Age 16 —

good memories of yester-year
caught on a camcorder to look at today.

— Age 61 —

when I catch a really big fish all by myself.

— Age 11 —

seeing a rainbow and knowing who to thank.

— Age 45 —

Happiness is...

knowing when your parents make a promise to you, they will always keep it no matter what.

— Age 22 —

being around nature, going on camping trips with my scout group.

— Age 12 —

having your two year-old granddaughter come to have lunch with you in the middle of the week.

— Age 55 —

Happiness is...

bike riding on a sunny day with my friends.

— Age 10 —

going to Six Flags and getting
to ride everything out there.

— Age 13 —

my son saying, "Mom, play fair.
Don't let me win."

— Age 34 —

my dad.

— Age 7 —

Happiness is...

going fishing with my granddaddy,
even if he wouldn't let me move a muscle.

— Age 9 —

knowing someone is always there
to depend on and lean on.

— Age 26 —

achieving goals, making it through
something you never thought you would, and
hot summer days with nothing to do.

— Age 17 —

Happiness is...

knowing you are special
to someone who cares about you.

— Age 21 —

being loved and appreciated by the
people you love and appreciate.

— Age 16 —

Life. Life is for the living
and I'm living it the very best I can,
and that makes me happy.

— Age 37 —

Happiness is...

getting through college
without failing a single subject.

— Age 22 —

being glad and feeling proud of yourself.

— Age 10 —

being healthy, because if you are
healthy then you are happy.

— Age 34 —

God's eternal gift.

— Age 56 —

Happiness is...

swinging on my swing set
and just having fun outside.

— Age 5 —

spending the night at my
grandmother's house.

— Age 8 —

singing Christmas carols at a nursing home
and watching the faces of the patients
light up with a smile.

— Age 18 —

Happiness is…

*my son, good health, my job,
and being able to be a good father
as well as a good worker.*

— Age 35 —

*eating at McDonald's and playing
on the play yard for as long as I want.*

— Age 6 —

*going to Disney World and
seeing Mickey Mouse.*

— Age 7 —

Happiness is...

a chocolate cookie with milk.

— Age 14 —

a Quarter Pounder with cheese.

— Age 16 —

having a day off from work
and visiting my children in school.

— Age 36 —

when you have a pocket full of money
that you can spend any way you want.

— Age 19 —

Happiness is...

the feeling I get after eating
a big juicy steak and fries.

— Age 32 —

being able to love yourself first
and then others.

— Age 20 —

an emotion that we all want
to feel every day.

— Age 18 —

Happiness is…

within yourself and
you have to find it for yourself.

— Age 55 —

a feeling of joy and pleasure, where
you are on top of the world. When you find
happiness hold it as long as you can,
it will not last forever.

— Age 39 —

living a fulfilled life and
having almost everything you want.

— Age 25 —

Happiness is...

being self confident.

— Age 15 —

my boyfriend calling me just to say hello.

— Age 24 —

getting flowers for no reason at all.

— Age 36 —

being asked to the prom on the first day it's announced.

— Age 16 —

Happiness is…

having Jesus in your life and
working hard at fulfilling your dreams.

— Age 17 —

having success in life and fun with friends.

— Age 28 —

the rebirth of life.

— Age 52 —

waking up to watch the sunrise and
hearing the birds sing.

— Age 45 —

Happiness is...

an ample supply of Reeses peanut butter cups and a tall glass of milk, when an overwhelming case of the munchies has taken control of your mind.

— Age 17 —

staying home from school and sleeping all day with your dog at your feet.

— Age 9 —

Jackson Hole, Wyoming.

— Age 22 —

Happiness is...

knowing who your friends really are.

— Age 24 —

love, fulfillment within yourself, success, and something very important.

— Age 35 —

when you get a test paper back and find out you passed it, instead of failing it like you had thought.

— Age 18 —

Happiness is...

going on a shopping spree with mom and she pays.

— Age 19 —

the most beautiful thing that anybody could have in their life.

— Age 32 —

falling asleep to the sound of rain hitting the window.

— Age 18 —

Happiness is…

peace of mind, never having
to worry about anything.

— Age 34 —

sunning on the beach with my boyfriend.

— Age 19 —

being blessed with love
and family who love me.

— Age 67 —

healthy children and my wife of 23 years.

— Age 54 —

Happiness is…

hugs and kisses at all times of the day.

— Age 22 —

being able to play golf all year round
if I want and being healthy.

— Age 43 —

a close relationship with God and family, and
being able to tell others about it.

— Age 36 —

being comfortable with life where I am today.

— Age 46 —

Happiness is…

when I saw my first grandchild for the first time, and knowing that he was healthy and well.

— Age 56 —

when my sister plays with me, and doesn't argue about what to play or how to play it.

— Age 12 —

seeing my cousins who live far away from me.

— Age 8 —

Happiness is…

financial security and exciting weekends.

— Age 30 —

not working, spending time with friends, and fishing on a sunny day.

— Age 67 —

competition, which brings out the best in all of us.

— Age 15 —

playing golf and shooting par on 18 holes.

— Age 39 —

Happiness is…

when you know you are needed, loved, and everyone cares.

— Age 23 —

being able to enjoy life day by day, and not be in any pain.

— Age 98 —

growing up in a small town like Tyrone and growing up to become a huge star.

— Age 16 —

when you are surfing on a killer wave about six feet tall and you make it all the way in.

— Age 21 —

hunting out in the woods without a telephone ringing or anyone bothering me.

— Age 51 —

galloping on horseback, riding a motorcycle, watching a storm come in with the ocean rolling toward me – it is a feeling of freedom and love of life.

— Age 24 —

Happiness is...

a cold drink on a hot summer day and a dip in the swimming pool.

— Age 19 —

that at this moment you are who you want to be.

— Age 16 —

yesterday's love feeling brand new today.

— Age 74 —

love and success in all that you do.

— Age 47 —

Happiness is…

a warm bubble bath at the end of a day of caring for my two children, preparing meals, going to P.T.A. meetings, speaking at a luncheon – just a few things that make up my day.

— Age 49 —

a good relationship with my whole family and my friends.

— Age 40 —

not ever pretending to be someone you're not.

— Age 17 —

Happiness is...

opening a shoe box at Christmas and finding my most wanted gift – a puppy in it.

— Age 11 —

sitting alone on a pier in the middle of a lake with good thoughts in my mind.

— Age 24 —

knowing that you've worked extremely hard for a goal and that you achieved it.

— Age 39 —

Happiness is...

reading every day and keeping busy.

— Age 88 —

arriving to the delivery room and being able to see the joy of my new baby being born.

— Age 33 —

being with friends and loved ones, having a good time without being stressed or worried.

— Age 22 —

making others happy around me.

— Age 92 —

Happiness is...

being content with the person you are
and the person you are trying to become.

— Age 16 —

having people care and love me,
and knowing how to show it.

— Age 27 —

not being afraid to sleep
in my own bed all night.

— Age 5 —

Happiness is...

if my real mom was back alive.

— Age 12 —

my sister tickling me and telling me that she loves me, even if I am her sister.

— Age 12 —

when my mom gives me a hug for no reason.

— Age 5 —

being able to play outside on a sunny day and having my mom watch me.

— Age 7 —

Happiness is…

seeing all my loved ones around me and seeing that they are happy.

— Age 82 —

like a spring day with all the beautiful flowers.

— Age 45 —

being able to relate to my mother about everything.

— Age 45 —

Happiness is...

watching a sick friend get well.

— Age 54 —

knowing that your parents are proud of you no matter what you do.

— Age 28 —

loving my neighbor and friends, and getting along with all races.

— Age 27 —

coloring.

— Age 4 —

Happiness is...

having the parents that I have.

— Age 15 —

living in a clean world with people who believe "do unto others as you would have them do unto you" is still fashionable.

— Age 36 —

like riding a roller coaster, you feel happier at the top than at the bottom.

— Age 15 —

Happiness is...

knowing one day there will be another place where there is no prejudice, no anger, no evil – only eternal love.

— Age 50 —

going to a friend's house and playing dolls.

— Age 6 —

alive with good health – seeing lovely people and having lots of friends.

— Age 66 —

Happiness is...

watching my grandson play baseball.

— Age 53 —

cuddling with my husband.

— Age 29 —

playing in a state softball tournament and tagging someone out at home plate, and looking over at my dad, my coach, and seeing him smile and talk about how good it was that I kept the other team from scoring.

— Age 17 —

Happiness is…

going to school and learning how to color.

— Age 6 —

playing bingo and doing crafts of all kinds.

— Age 88 —

my little girl calling me mommy.

— Age 32 —

the day I met my husband and fell in love.

— Age 83 —

Happiness is...

playing with friends who like me and having a snack.

— Age 7 —

after-school hours when I don't have to study or do house work.

— Age 12 —

seeing a child's face light up when they see Santa Claus for the first time.

— Age 33 —

Happiness is...

being married, and having children,
and watching them grow.

— Age 34 —

the feeling of emotions that are true.

— Age 17 —

seeing a shared love in another's eyes.

— Age 31 —

going outside and watching the butterflies
and trying to catch one in my hand.

— Age 8 —

Happiness is…

a day off from work so I can just play with my children and have fun.

— Age 33 —

love for fellow man and thanking God that I have lived to be seventy.

— Age 70 —

going out to the mall and hanging out with my friends, and riding my pony.

— Age 11 —

someone to love you and share love with, children to be proud of, having Christ in my life, and harmony.

— Age 66 —

not being on a schedule and having senior citizens benefits when I am young.

— Age 55 —

lots of things, like having Stephenia come over and us talking on the phone in the closet.

— Age 14 —

Happiness is...

looking for the good, rather than the bad, in people, a positive attitude.

— Age 30 —

not giving up.

— Age 24 —

driving one of America's fine classics.

— Age 35 —

when you see the sky blue, the clouds white, and you know that you are alive.

— Age 66 —

Happiness is...

staying in a log cabin in the mountains and watching the fire burn in the fireplace with someone special.

— Age 25 —

having God in my life and sharing it with others.

— Age 50 —

quality time with people I love and care about the most.

— Age 20 —

Happiness is…

peace among all people.

— Age 54 —

going to sleep at night, waking up the next morning, and knowing you made it on earth another day.

— Age 51 —

moonlight on the beach and hearing the ocean roll in.

— Age 29 —

Happiness is…

knowing you'll have a chance of going to heaven when you die.

— Age 74 —

knowing that you are loved unconditionally.

— Age 41 —

living alone on a yacht in the Gulf of Mexico.

— Age 35 —

going to a Chicago Cubs game with my dad.

— Age 15 —

Happiness is...

finding money in my pocket that I didn't know was there.

— Age 16 —

making my first touchdown.

— Age 16 —

knowing I have passed all my classes.

— Age 15 —

seeing a friend you haven't seen in a long time and remembering old times.

— Age 66 —

Happiness is...

finally getting to go on that cruise that I have been wanting to take since I was in high school.

— Age 68 —

who can define happiness?

— Age 45 —

having all the Coke I want and all I can eat for two years.

— Age 10 —

Happiness is...

my whole family pulling together and never holding a grudge.

— Age 35 —

feeling love all around me.

— Age 87 —

the way my mother raised me.

— Age 26 —

realizing that I have wrinkles and that I don't care.

— Age 68 —

Happiness is…

staying after school three days a week for marching band practice.

— Age 15 —

listening to my grandmother sing old songs to me while we are riding on a long trip.

— Age 33 —

jumping in the balls at McDonalds.

— Age 3 —

being married to my very best friend.

— Age 28 —

Happiness is...

knowing how to forgive.

— Age 48 —

finding two toys in the bottom of a cereal box.

— Age 7 —

being able to do and buy for others without disfurnishing yourself.

— Age 66 —

turning eighteen.

— Age 17 —

Happiness is...

to have your first book accepted by a publisher.

— Age 66 —

when you beat someone at their own game.

— Age 45 —

when you find out there is nothing left in your world, and your faithful dog Rover comes up and licks your hand.

— Age 20 —

Happiness is...

being accepted in a new school by your peers on the very first day.

— Age 15 —

when you try and succeed at something you thought you could never do.

— Age 15 —

seeing the surprise on a bride's face when she realizes the bird seed being thrown went into her mouth.

— Age 49 —

Happiness is...

waking up and seeing the sunshine coming through your window, and feeling that you are loved.

— Age 34 —

feeling rich and funny.

— Age 22 —

reluctantly going on a cruise with a group of friends and finding you are not afraid after all, even though you can't swim.

— Age 55 —

Happiness is…

sharing God's greatest gift with others – love.

— Age 45 —

waking up to the fresh smell of the crisp country air, and knowing that you can spend the whole day with the one you love.

— Age 25 —

when you reach a point in your life when you realize – this is my life and I am responsible for making it happy.

— Age 65 —

Happiness is...

playing in the snow.

— Age 8 —

living life to the fullest, knowing you have world peace and that you live in a clean environment.

— Age 64 —

the ability to experience and enjoy the world around you.

— Age 15 —

the joy of living and having food, shelter, clothes, and being loved.

— Age 46 —

a walk in the park with the birds flying over a church in October.

— Age 34 —

being on the beach in the Bahamas on a hot summer's day, listening to people laughing, hearing the water, getting a good tan.

— Age 24 —

Happiness is...

finding a front row parking space at the mall.

— Age 55 —

a feeling that comes from within,
not knowing what is coming up next,
and letting everything be a surprise.

— Age 37 —

when your teacher moves away...
far away...very far away!

— Age 15 —

Happiness is...

going to the store and
only getting what is on your list.

— Age 22 —

watching my sister when she throws
the bowling ball, forgets to turn loose,
and goes down the lane with the ball.

— Age 12 —

giving the food you hate to your dog
under the table without getting caught.

— Age 15 —

Happiness is...

going to the doctor and him saying "NO CHARGE."

— Age 40 —

a policeman only giving me a warning ticket when he pulls me over.

— Age 22 —

getting a call from Ed McMahon and him saying, "You have just won ten million dollars!"

— Age 45 —

staying on a diet long enough
to lose the weight that you want.

— Age 38 —

saying I didn't do it and
everybody believing me.

— Age 12 —

your neighbor finally putting
his bulldog on a leash.

— Age 41 —

Happiness is...

learning how to keep my body on top of the water instead of on the bottom, when I float.

— Age 67 —

finding out that my car, which I thought was broken down, was only out of gas.

— Age 32 —

going to the dentist and him saying, "No cavities."

— Age 19 —

Happiness is...

having a hobby I can make money off of.

— Age 24 —

seeing two boats come to your aid when you are trying to row your pontoon boat back to the dock.

— Age 44 —

hitting the jackpot in Vegas.

— Age 35 —

the first day of spring.

— Age 25 —

Happiness is...

driving into your garage moments before a storm hits.

— Age 56 —

the plumber saying, "It's not your pipes leaking, it's the city's pipes."

— Age 39 —

waking from a bad dream to realize it was only a dream.

— Age 12 —

Happiness is...

giving a baby shower and have thirty people attend.

— Age 32 —

not getting any duplicates in your wedding gifts.

— Age 29 —

being chosen "Senior Citizen of the Year" when you are eighty five.

— Age 85 —

Happiness is…

finally being tall enough to reach the pool table and being able to use a cue stick.

— Age 8 —

being able to go on a date without a chaperon.

— Age 17 —

not having to say, "Don't spill your milk."

— Age 34 —

bowling a perfect three hundred game.

— Age 53 —

Happiness is...

my mom letting me lick the spoon and clean the bowl after she made a cake.

— Age 5 —

watching the mama ducks and her babies swimming in the lake.

— Age 8 —

learning how to operate my new computer and make it do what I want it to do, instead of what it wants.

— Age 23 —

Happiness is...

going to the zoo and watching the monkeys make faces at all the people watching them.

— Age 19 —

living long enough, yet feeling young enough to enjoy four great grandchildren.

— Age 67 —

riding my horse.

— Age 13 —

getting a raise at work.

— Age 34 —

Happiness is…

my doctor saying, "No you are NOT pregnant."

— Age 40 —

going to Upton's two day sale.

— Age 24 —

my husband saying, "I'll love you forever and a day."

— Age 55 —

Dear Reader,

If this book has given you a happy moment, we are thankful.

Sharon and Ollie

Happiness is…

Happiness is...

Happiness is…

Happiness is...